Quick & Creative
Reading Response Activities

More Than 60 Sensational Make-and-Learn Activities to Help Kids Respond Meaningfully to What They Read

BY JANE FOWLER AND STEPHANIE NEWLON

SCHOLASTIC
PROFESSIONAL BOOKS

NEW YORK • TORONTO • LONDON • AUCKLAND • SYDNEY
MEXICO CITY • NEW DELHI • HONG KONG • BUENOS AIRES

This book is dedicated to our families, who have found ways to be understanding and tolerant of the many hours we have spent creating, preparing, and sharing our ideas with fellow educators near and far.
Thank you, we love you.

Acknowledgments

We would like to take this opportunity to acknowledge the students in our classrooms. Over the years, they have taken our ideas and expanded and altered them to create new learning possibilities. What an exciting and rewarding experience this has been.
Yes, learning and teaching can be fun!

Interior design by **Holly Grundon**
Cover design by **Jim Sarfati**
Interior art by **James Hale**

ISBN: 0-439-09845-9

A B C D E F G H I J K L M N O P Q R S T U V W X Y Z

Contents

Introduction

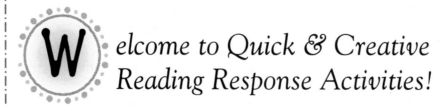

elcome to Quick & Creative Reading Response Activities!

Reading is a solitary activity. At the same time, we know that encouraging kids to talk about books—to share their thoughts and interpretations with others in interactive and creative ways—builds comprehension. The activities in this book help children do just that!

Increasing comprehension adds joy and pleasure to the reading experience. The reading response activities you'll find in these pages help children reflect upon any book they've read, forming the foundation for further questioning and discussion.

Though the activities may originate as nonverbal, they often lead to more discussion. Sharing these activities boosts the confidence of reluctant readers and encourages them to take part in group discussions. Sharing these projects is also valuable both for the listener and the child who is participating. The child develops confidence, the audience develops listening skills—and everyone becomes aware of one another's appreciation and interpretation of literature. Sharing develops a spirit of community!

In our classrooms, we've found that activities like these build a love and appreciation of literature—and make teaching and learning more enjoyable for all. These activities will promote literal comprehension and build skills in explicit recognition and recall. They'll help children organize their ideas and information, and help them use this information as an experience base in judging literature. And besides ... they're lots of fun!

— *Jane Fowler & Stephanie Newlon*

Using This Book

For each letter of the alphabet, you'll find one or more reading response activities that can be used with any book. You might:

- let children choose their own projects (introduce several activities and encourage children to choose among them), or assign the whole group the same project.

- invite children to do the projects as book reports, or as extensions of traditional book reports.

- have children work in small groups to complete a project together.

- have children stand in front of the group to share their work when finished, explaining what they've done and how it relates to the piece of literature.

- list several of the projects (with instructions) on chart paper and display at a learning center, so that kids can choose and complete them during center time.

- assign the projects as homework or as family projects.

- invite children to share an "alphabet" of responses at open house. Display and label a response activity for each letter of the alphabet, and have children share their work as families visit the classroom.

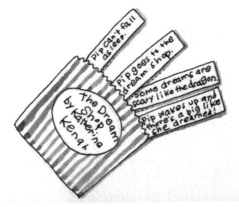

Accordion Books

Divide the class into groups of three to five students. The group members then divide the story into the number of people in the group (for instance, if there are four people in the group, they divide the story into four parts). Then, each child explains what happened first, second, third and last in the book. Each member of the group is responsible for summarizing and illustrating their part of the story on a blank piece of white paper. When complete, children lay their papers side by side and tape them together. They then fan-fold the pages to create an accordion book, and share their story with the rest of the class.

A-mazing Adventures

Draw attention to the adventure and action in any book! Provide children with a copy of "A-mazing A" (page 32). Encourage them to list four adventures or actions from the story. Have them color their A, and add symbols that relate to the story. Then, children cut out the letters and punch a hole in the top. Hang the A's from the ceiling—you'll have one action-packed room!

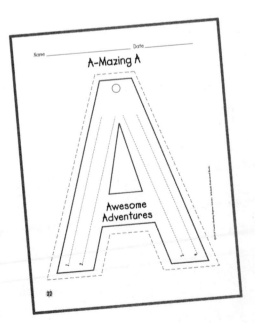

Brown Bag Backdrops

Help children use small brown paper lunch bags as backdrops for stick puppets. Encourage children to decorate their bags with an appropriate scene from a story and then create and color stick puppets (representing characters from the story), using index cards, tape, and craft sticks. The puppets can be stored in the bags. Children will build oral communication skills by retelling a story using their bags and puppets.

Book Bag Puppets

Use brown paper lunch bags to create book reports! Use this activity to retell a story (or generate a new story based on the original story's characters or concepts). Turn the bag upside down. Use the rectangle at top for a character portrait and staple a written summary onto the body of the bag (see right). Children will find they've made a puppet accompanied by a small book!

The Dog and the Dino
Illustrated by Tanya. There was once a dog in town and her name was Princess. She was waiting around the block when suddenly she heard a fire engine.

Character Cash

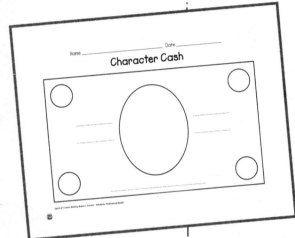

Have children choose a character from a story they've read. Every character becomes a millionaire with this activity! Provide each child with a copy of page 33 to create currency for their character. (Remind children what is on U.S. currency: symbols representing important people and places, different numerals, dates, and so on.) Encourage children to draw a picture of their character, and to add symbols to the front and back to represent important qualities of the character. Children might add titles by the same author, the character's city or town, and so on. Numerals might represent the character's age. You might even have children cut out their character cash, then work in small groups to create math problems with the bills!

Character Cards

Bring characters to life with crayons and large index cards. First, have children create an easel to showcase these character cards. Fold an index card in half and cut on the open side to form the letter L (see below). Children can decorate their easels with small symbols from the story. Then, have them use another index card to draw a picture of their favorite character from a book and write a description of the character on the back (these descriptions may include physical characteristics, likes, dislikes, personality traits, goals, problems, family, and friends). The character cards fit on the easel for easy display. Children can then "introduce" their character in small groups or to the whole class.

Design and Decorate

Provide sheets of white butcher paper and encourage children to use crayons or markers to design and decorate a home or room for a character in a story. Mention that they should think about their character carefully to know what he or she would want to have in his or her room or house. Children should be able to explain why they created certain things in the room and how they reflect the character, based on information in the story. This provides a wonderful opportunity to observe children's insight into a character! Children can give "tours" of the house or room to the rest of the group.

Diary

A classroom diary is an excellent comprehension strategy to use following a daily read-aloud. Ask a different child to write an entry in a class notebook every day. Children should summarize the story in a few sentences, and write a comment about the plot or character development. If children illustrate the entries, you will have a delightful class book that kids can enjoy over and over again. These entries can be used to revisit the many characters and stories you've enjoyed each day. This makes an impressive display for classroom visitors and parents. (Children can also keep individual book diaries using small composition books kept in their own desks, then share them with small groups or the whole class.)

Event Cards

Sequencing events in a story is a vital element in comprehension — and this activity provides students with the opportunity to do just that. Give students three or four index cards in a variety of colors. Children draw on one side of the card and write the events of a story on the other side, telling what happened first, next, and last. They then exchange card sets with a partner, who attempts to put them in the correct order. Children check each other's work (they might hide a small number noting the correct sequence on the back of each card as a self-checking device).

E-mails

Everyone gets e-mails; why not the characters of your favorite books? Have children make up imaginary e-mail addresses for their characters. Ask, *How do people decide on e-mail addresses, anyway? What would be a good e-mail address for your character, and why?* You might print out a blank e-mail template and copy it for children to write on. They can write a message to their character, or write it as though they were the character.

Filmstrips

Have children use adding machine tape to re-create the most exciting part of the story. On the tape, they should draw pictures and write about the events of the story in order. (These "filmstrips" can also be used to list vocabulary or spelling words.) They can be rolled up and kept in empty toilet paper rolls that have been decorated with symbols from the story. The completed tubes can be collected and kept in shoe boxes (labeled "adventure books," "fantasy books," "compound words," "vocabulary words," "favorite characters," "spelling words we know," and so on) for independent viewing.

Fun Facts

Children can record facts from a nonfiction story on index cards and hang them around the room, providing an instant resource center for reports. In small groups, students can research a selected topic and record facts on index cards. They can then draw or paint a large figure and hang the cards together in groups of four or five. For instance, if children read a story about a whale, they can make a large whale from posterboard or construction paper and attach these fact cards with yarn to the whale's body. Hang the whale from the ceiling or bulletin board for easy reference.

Fun Fax

Communication comes alive in your classroom with your own fax machine! Make a pretend fax machine from an empty cereal box. Cover and decorate it to look like a fax machine (cut a slit at each end where papers can pass through). Discuss the purposes and uses of a fax machine, then encourage children to "fax" a message to a character in a story! These messages can be read aloud and answered as a group or individually. Collect the faxes and their responses in a folder entitled "Fabulous Faxes."

French Fry Facts

Discuss the difference between fact and opinion. Provide each child with a white paper lunch bag (cut with pinking shears to resemble a french fry bag) and four strips of yellow paper (french fries), two by six inches long. Encourage children to write down four facts from a story (such as setting, characters, problem, and solutions, or what happened first, second, third, and last in the story). Then have them write sentences on the french fries and put them in the white sack!

Great Graphs

Create a graph with two columns: questions and answers. Choose questions that relate to your spelling, grammar, or vocabulary lessons and have children go back to a chosen story or chapter and find the answers. For instance, *How many short a words can you find in the story? How many words with five letters on page 6? How many new vocabulary words can you find? How many words can you find on page 6 that start with th-?* Have children record the numbers to create a class graph.

Gloves

Have each child trace his or her hand onto a plain piece of white paper and cut it out. On the palm, children should record the title and author name, then write different events from the story on each finger. Then have them glue the hands onto colored construction paper and display them on a bulletin board. (If you do this during cold weather, you might entitle the display "Warm Up Your Hands With a Good Book!")

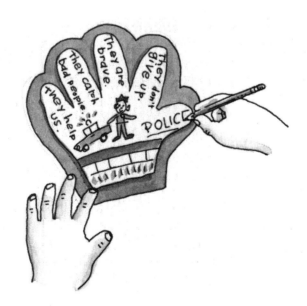

High-Five Hands

Have each child trace his or her hand onto a plain piece of paper. On the palm, children can write a character's name. On each finger, they can write a reason their character deserves a "high five"! Cut out the hands, mount them on construction paper, and display them on a bulletin board labeled "Give Reading a High Five!"

Hugs for the Characters

Every character deserves a hug! Copy page 34 for each child and spread the hugs around as children fill in the hearts with reasons their character needs a hug. Children then color and cut them out to create a bulletin board entitled "Everyone Deserves a Hug."

If I Were . . .

Get the creative juices flowing as you ask children to step into the character of a book! Copy page 35 for each child and help him or her complete it. Children describe what they would do if they were the character, and why. When completed, they can share their ideas with the class. These "If I Were..." sentence stems can also be used as interview questions, as children ask each other to share other events in the story and what they would have done.

It Made Sense

Have each child create a sense chart: two columns of five rows, one for each sense (seeing, tasting, hearing, smelling, touching). Choose a story, and encourage children to fill in the chart next to the appropriate senses. (For instance, in *Charlie and the Chocolate Factory*, Charlie smells chocolate, tastes the gobstopper, sees Oompa-Loompas, and so on.) The completed charts may be used as a brainstorming tool prior to writing a paragraph describing a character or an incident he or she was involved in. These character charts may also be compared with other projects on characters in the room. It will "make sense" to use these as as a unique comprehension tool!

Jumbo Trading Cards

Share a variety of trading cards with the group. Discuss the information found on the cards, then encourage children to create a "Jumbo Trading Card" for their favorite character. Provide each child with a copy of page 36 and help them fill in the blanks and draw and color a favorite character. Then, play a game in which a child reads the character's information and the class guesses the character. Exchanging and sharing these character cards in small groups is a great way to encourage small-group discussion.

Kites

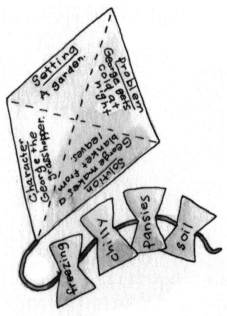

Give each child a diamond-shaped piece of construction paper and tell the group they are going to make a kite that tells a story. First, have them fold the paper in half twice, to create four triangles. The kite will become a story map for the setting, character, problem, and solution! Use yarn and ribbon to create a tail for the kite—and tie on important vocabulary words (or simply favorite words that children choose). Encourage students to retell the story as they "fly" (show to the group) their kite.

Lightbulb Lab

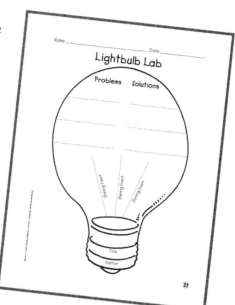

Copy page 37 for each child. On the "shining events" lines, children write three important events from a story. Then they write down three problems in the story on one side of the bulb and three corresponding solutions on the other side. They can then color their bulbs. Watch faces light up with learning!

Literacy Times

What better way to review question words (Who, What, Where, When, Why and How), than with your own *Literacy Times*? Have children form five groups and assign each group a section of the paper (front page, sports, comics, world news, and even classified). Using information from a chosen book, each group writes an article for the *Literacy Times*. This activity may also be done individually, with each child creating his or her own front page.

Mailboxes

Have children design mailboxes for a character, using shoe boxes or empty oatmeal containers. Children can cover the boxes and decorate them with symbols from the story that reflect the character or storyline. Invite children to write letters or postcards to the characters (or from their character to the class), and deliver them to the correct mailboxes. You might discuss the postal system at this time. The letters and postcards can be shared at "mail call."

Mood-o-Meter

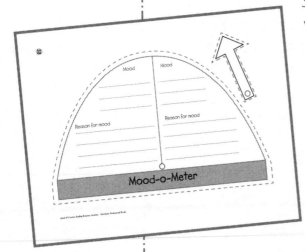

What kind of mood is each child's character in in the chapter he or she is reading? How about the next? Have children read the character's mood daily with your own Mood-o-Meter. Copy page 38 for each child. Have children choose a mood that was experienced by a character in the story and write it on the top edge of the "meter." Children can write examples from the story that illustrate why the character was in that mood. On the other side of the meter, students write another mood and explain in writing the reason for the character's mood. Using a brad and a small arrow, children can move the arrow back and forth as the character's mood changes. Be "meter readers," as each child shares his or her character's changing moods.

Notable Necklaces

Give each child several index cards. On the back of each card, have children describe a different character from a story and draw the character's picture on the front. Then they can punch holes and string the cards on a piece of yarn, wearing it as a necklace as they introduce their whole cast of characters to their classmates.

On Board

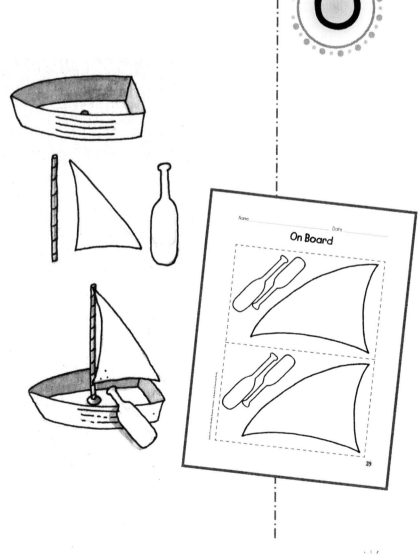

Students set sail with stories! Provide an empty, clean french fry "boat" for each child (ask a local restaurant to donate, or check the paper plate aisle in your supermarket). Create a sail for each boat by providing every two children with a copy of page 39 (so that each child gets one sail shape and two oars). Students then write a problem from a story on the sail and solutions on the oars. Children decorate the outside of the boat with the book title and author's name. Have them attach the sail to the boat, using a straw or small craft stick that has been poked through the bottom of the boat. Don't worry about any sinking ships here! Children will enjoy sailing away with this new literature strategy.

Problem-Solving Predictions

Provide each child with an empty paper towel roll, a plain piece of paper to cover the roll, and a large index card on which they draw the main character of a chosen story. Have them decorate the paper and use it to cover the roll. At some point in a given story where a problem or a chance to make a prediction occurs, have them stop reading! Encourage children to write on a separate half sheet of paper either their prediction of what will happen, or the solution to the character's

problem. Then have them roll up their paper and put it in the paper towel roll. Encourage class members to share their predictions or solutions before finishing the story.

Puzzle Cards

Provide children with large index cards, and encourage them to draw a picture of a character on one half of the card and details describing the character on the other half. They then cut the index card in half (similar to the patterns on a jigsaw puzzle). Scatter the cards on a table with a small group. Children can read the cards and try to match the picture with the description. If the puzzle fits, it's a match!

Personal Picture Frames

Display pictures of favorite characters children have drawn throughout your classroom as each child shares his or her favorite characters. Use a five-by-seven index card for a frame (cut out the inside of the card in either an oval or rectangular shape). Children should decorate these frames with words and symbols that depict the character. Then have children add a picture of the character.

Playtime

Divide the class into groups of four and give each group a copy of page 40 (all children in each group should have read, or listened to you read aloud, the same book). Provide each group with 10 index cards cut in half; these will become the game cards. Encourage children to create five questions each about the setting, characters, problems, or solutions of the book (one question per card). Place the cards near the game board. Children will need game markers and a die. They roll to see who goes first (highest number). That child then reads and answers a question card; a correct answer allows them to move again.

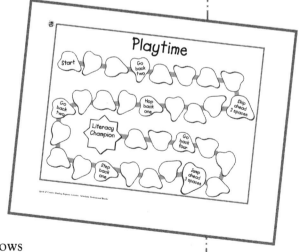

Quilt Talk

Children can create a class collaborative quilt after they read a story. Divide the class into six small groups. Each group is assigned one of the following: title, author, characters, beginning/middle/end of story, new vocabulary, and favorite part of the story. Children decorate the quilt squares with pictures, symbols, or sentences drawn on index cards that describe or depict these elements of the story. Each quilt square may be glued onto different-colored construction paper. Assemble the quilt as each group shares its square.

Rock 'n' Roll

Do you have any composers in your classroom? Find out by providing paper, pencils and some musical instruments. Invite children to create a new song to go along with their favorite story, or a song for their favorite character. These songs can be sung to familiar tunes, such as "Row, Row, Row Your Boat" or "Twinkle, Twinkle, Little Star."

Stationery

Provide children with a variety of paper in all sizes, textures, colors and shapes. Invite them to create stationery for their favorite characters. They might decorate paper with a border of symbols that represent the characters or incidents of the story (stationery for one of the Three Little Pigs, for instance, may be decorated with a border of bricks, sticks, and straw). This stationery can be used as children "become" the characters, writing a letter to a real-life friend as if it came from their character.

Superhero Capes

Every character becomes a superhero with this activity, which works best with strong characters in the story. Using the cape outline on page 41, students decorate their character cape with symbols and short sentences describing how the character shows strength. Cut out and display the capes on a bulletin board entitled "Our Superheroes." Superman will be in fine company once children complete this activity!

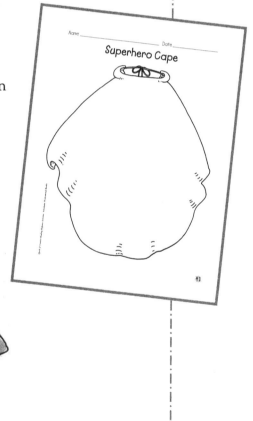

T-Shirts

Children can design a shirt for a character on a piece of paper cut in the shape of a T-shirt. Invite children to decorate their T-shirts to reflect the character's personality and interests. (These T-shirts can also be used across the curriculum and can become a place to display math facts, symbols for a report on a U.S. state report, or words starting with the same sounds.) Hang shirts from a clothesline with clothespins!

Tea Bags

Children can record the problems and solutions of a story on individual tea bags made from index cards, string, and tracing paper. Cut an index card into the shape of a tea bag (cut the top corners off). Save a small part of the card to make the tag that goes on the other end of the string. Children record the problem on the larger part (the bag itself) and the solution on the smaller square. Children might also illustrate the problem on the tea bag. Cover the tea bag with the tracing paper to make it

look authentic, and attach the string to the bag and the tag to the string. Cut out large teacups from construction paper and cut a slit in which to place the tea bag. Display on a bulletin board with a caption such as "Tea-riffic Stories"!

Umbrellas

Children reflect on the strength of their character as they complete the umbrella outline (page 42). On the handle of the umbrella, have children list traits of a main character from a story they like. Then have them fill the umbrella itself with problems the character is facing. Point out that a character's strengths can help him or her handle the problems. Children may also decorate their umbrella with symbols, to make each umbrella a sight to behold. Now all you need is a little rain!

V Is for Vacation

Create a passport for a character! Copy pages 43-44 (so that the copies are two-sided) for each child. Using information from a favorite story, children determine where they would like their character to go on vacation. They can draw a picture of the character on the inside, add biographical information, and write a short paragraph suggesting the vacation destination for their character. They might also decorate the outside of the passport with symbols that represent the character. Display on a bulletin board entitled "Take a Trip With a Book!"

Passport for
_____

Country

Vests

Help children create vests for their favorite characters in a story. Cut large brown paper grocery bags into vests (cut neck and armholes and cut open the front of the "vest"). Then have children add symbols or words representing their character. They can wear the vests as they describe their character to the group.

Wonder Wands

Children can use a "magic wand" to interview one another about their thoughts on a story the class has read. The wand can be as simple as a paper towel tube with a rolled-up ball of tinfoil stuck into one end, or a large spoon or chalkboard pointer. Have children take turns walking around the room and asking other students questions, using the wand as a microphone. Comments might be recorded using a sentence frame: _____ wonders _____ . ("Brian wonders what Verdi will do next.")

Watch the Character Change

Many children enjoy wearing a watch! Make time fly as students create a paper watch for their favorite character. Have children draw their character in the face of the watch (copy page 45 for each child). On one strap, children should write the traits of the character in the beginning of the book, and on the other strap, how the character changed by the end of the story. Or, they can write problems on one strap and solutions on the other. Everyone will be telling "timely" stories of their character with this activity!

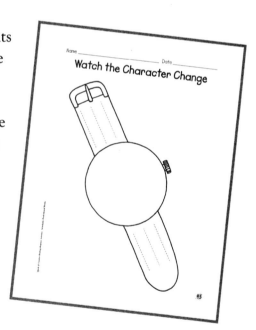

Name _____ Date _____
Watch the Character Change

45

X-rays

What is inside a character's house? A character's diary? A character's heart or mind? A character's pocket? Read a story to the class and have "story doctors" speculate on these topics. Students should write down questions on index cards for the story doctor and submit them to his or her office for evaluation. Encourage the doctors to review the story and create an "X-ray" picture of their answer. For instance, if the question on the card is "What is in Willy Wonka's pocket?" the X-ray might depict a list of children's names and secret candy recipes.

X-tra, X-tra, Read All About It!

Children can write articles recording the important events of a story. Collect the articles and display them on a bulletin board (covered with newspapers as a background).

You Be the Character

Children "step into character" by creating headbands that represent a character! Simple headbands can be made from construction paper strips cut to fit around a child's head. Children draw, color, and cut out the selected character and attach it to the strip. You might also use butcher paper to create a life-size character: Draw and color the character on the paper. Don't forget to cut a hole in the paper so that the child can put his or her face through! In addition, you can use a paper plate to create a mask that resembles the character's face (add string so that children can wear the masks). Any of these props can be used as the student shares a story with the class, or is interviewed by classmates regarding his or her part in the story.

Yesterday

Children can record the daily events of their favorite character using the "Yesterday, Today, Tomorrow" sheet (copy page 46 for each child). First, discuss with the group what a day planner is used for. Using information from the story, children fill in the "plans" of the character in the appropriate space. Children will revisit and review the story as they search for the daily events of their character, as well as make predictions about what the character might do in the future.

Zip!

Children can use a one-minute timer as they "zip" through the story they've read, retelling a friend the most important information. They can also time themselves as they write as many facts, events, characters, or vocabulary words as they can remember from the story.

Student
Pages

Name _____ Date _____

A-Mazing A

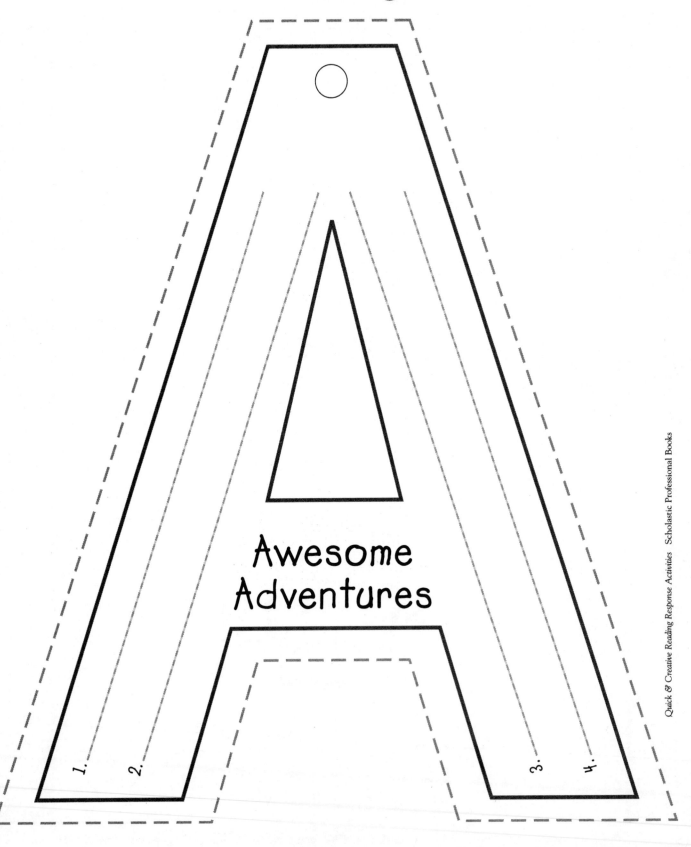

Awesome
Adventures

1.

2.

3.

4.

Quick & Creative Reading Response Activities Scholastic Professional Books

Name _____

Character Cash

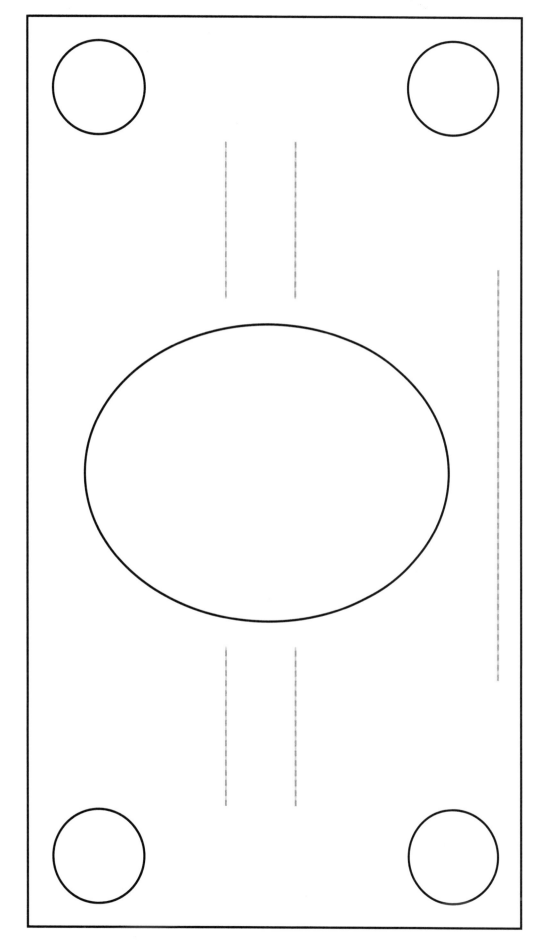

Name _____ Date _____

Hugs for the Character

deserves a hug because

Another hug for

because

One big hug for

because

Quick & Creative Reading Response Activities   Scholastic Professional Books

If I Were...

If I were _____,

I would _____

_____

_____.

I would also _____

_____

_____

_____

Jumbo Trading Card

Character Card

Name: _____

Book Title:

_____

Author:

_____

Character's Age:

_____

Lives in:

_____

Likes: _____

Dislikes: _____

Friends/Family: _____

Quick & Creative Reading Response Activities   Scholastic Professional Books

Lightbulb Lab

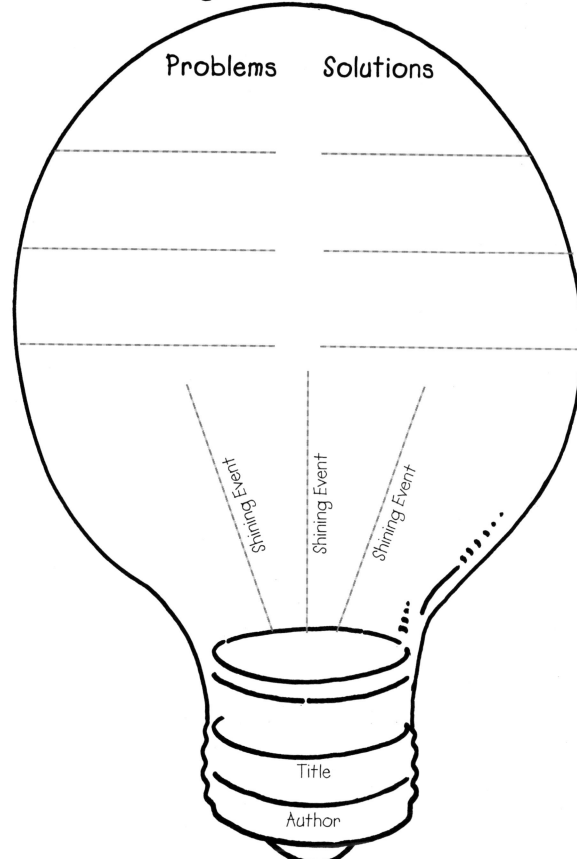

Problems   Solutions

Shining Event   Shining Event   Shining Event

Title

Author

Mood-o-Meter

Mood

Mood

Reason for mood

Reason for mood

Quick & Creative Reading Response Activities Scholastic Professional Books

On Board

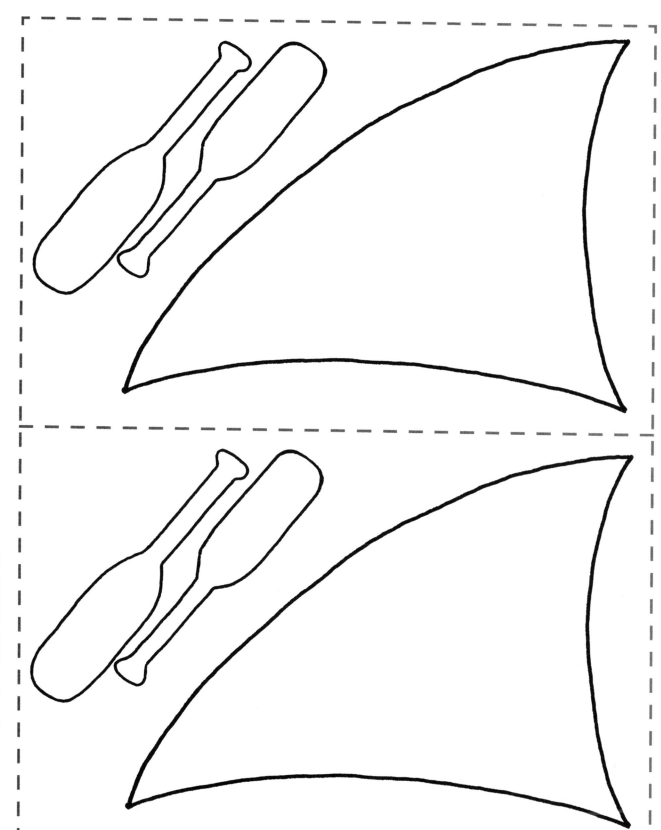

Playtime

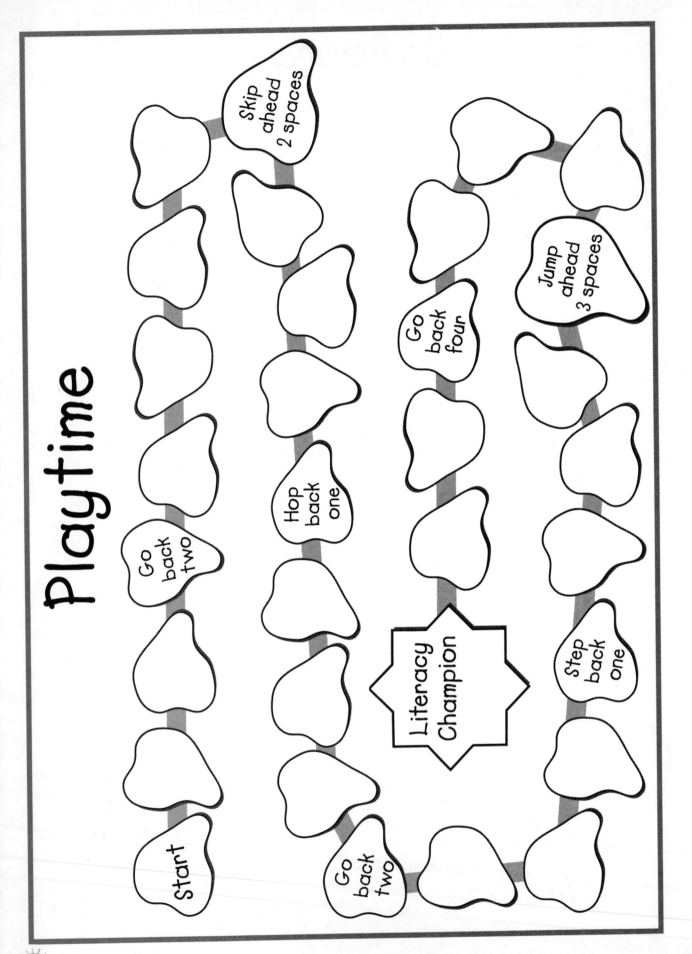

Start

Go back two

Skip ahead 2 spaces

Hop back one

Go back four

Jump ahead 3 spaces

Go back two

Literacy Champion

Step back one

Quick & Creative Reading Response Activities Scholastic Professional Books

Superhero Cape

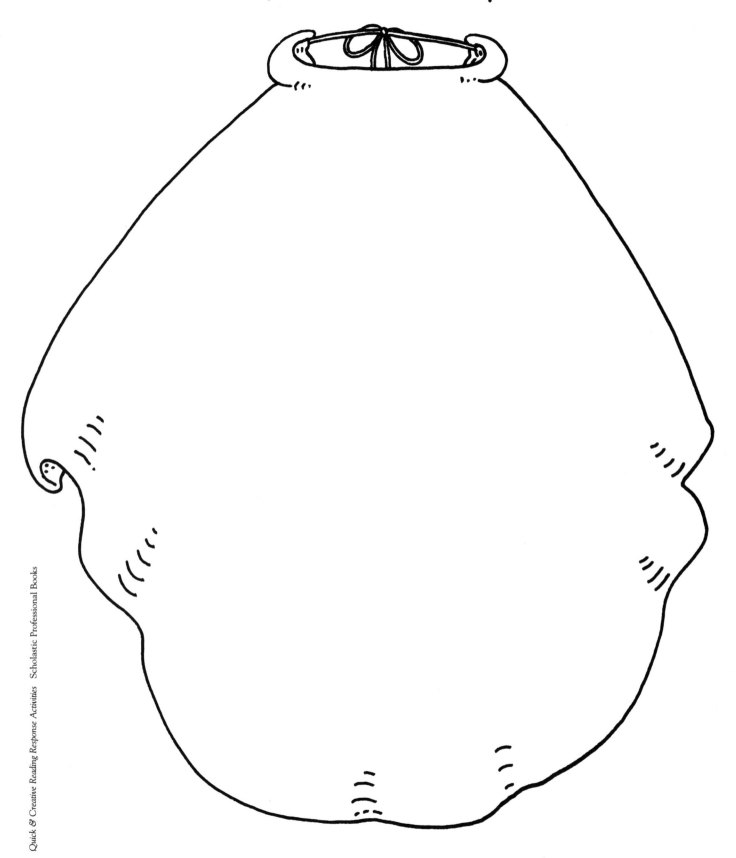

Character Umbrella

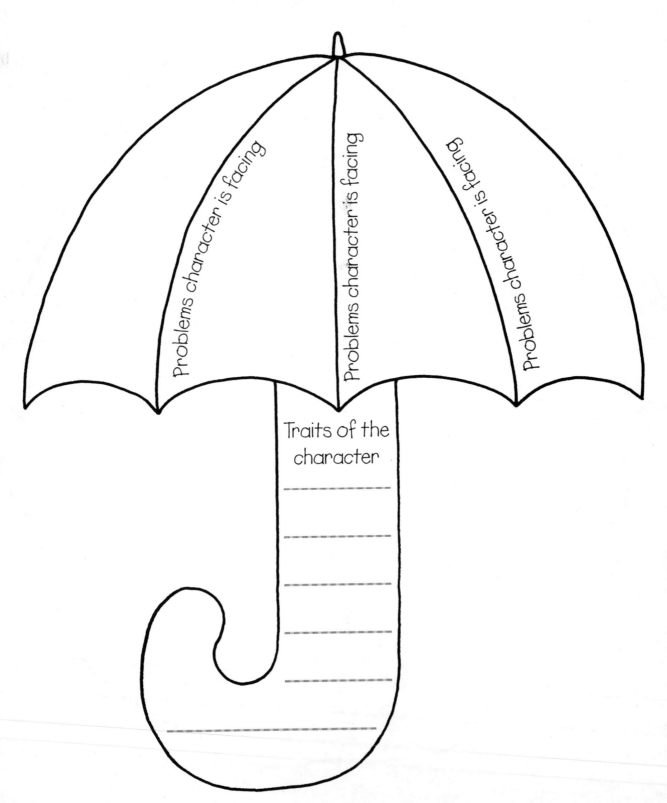

Problems character is facing

Problems character is facing

Problems character is facing

Traits of the
character

_____

_____

_____

_____

_____

_____

Quick & Creative Reading Response Activities   Scholastic Professional Books

Passport
for

_____

Country

fold here

should

go to

because

_____

_____

_____

_____

_____

_____

_____

_____

_____

_____

_____

fold here

Name:

Date of Birth:

Address:

Hair:

Eyes:

Name _____ Date _____

Watch the Character Change

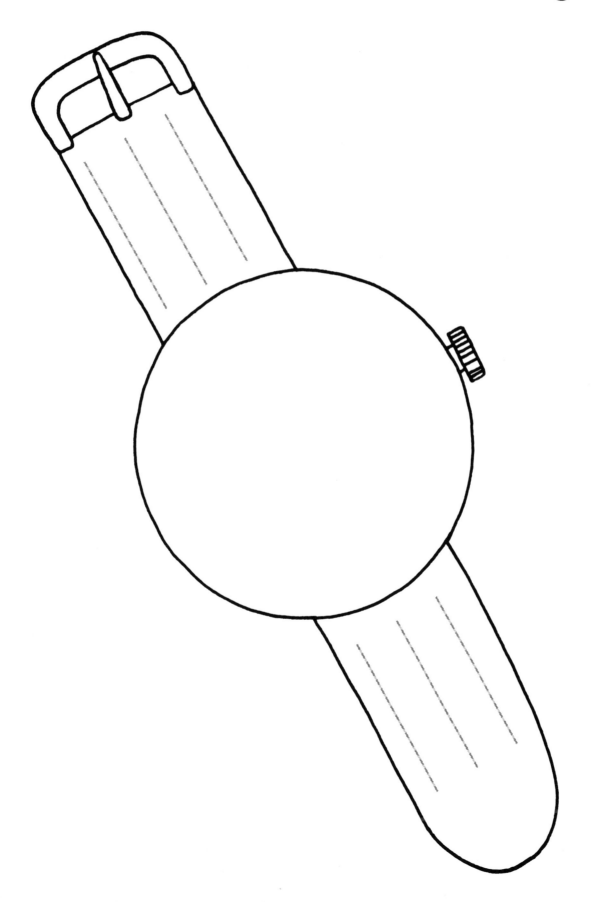

Day Planner

	Yesterday	Today	Tomorrow
Morning			
Afternoon			
Evening			

Quick & Creative Reading Response Activities Scholastic Professional Books

Notes

A B C D E F G H I J K L M N O P Q R S T U V W X Y Z

Notes

_____

_____

_____

_____

_____

_____

_____

_____

_____

_____

_____

_____

_____

_____

_____

_____

_____

_____